AMERICAN COMMUNITIES

We Live in the COUNTRY

Mary Austen

PowerKiDS press

New York

Published in 2016 by The Rosen Publishing Group, Inc.
29 East 21st Street, New York, NY 10010

First Edition

Editor: Katie Kawa
Book Design: Reann Nye

Photo Credits: Cover, pp. 3–24 (background texture) Evgeny Karandaev/Shutterstock.com; cover Sahani Photography/Shutterstock.com; p. 5 Kzenon/Shutterstock.com; p. 6 cdrin/Shutterstock.com; p. 9 (country) Francesco Ferrarini/Shutterstock.com; p. 9 (city) Manamana/Shutterstock.com; p. 10 WDG Photo/Shutterstock.com; p. 13 nata-lunata/Shutterstock.com; pp. 14, 24 (ranch) MaxyM/Shutterstock.com; p. 17 Ozerov Alexander/Shutterstock.com; p. 18 mlorenz/Shutterstock.com; pp. 21, 24 (field mouse) davemhuntphotography/Shutterstock.com; p. 22 Jon Bilous/Shutterstock.com.

Cataloging-in-Publication Data

Austen, Mary.
We live in the country / by Mary Austen.
p. cm. — (American communities)
Includes index.
ISBN 978-1-5081-4205-8 (pbk.)
ISBN 978-1-5081-4206-5 (6-pack)
ISBN 978-1-5081-4207-2 (library binding)
1. Country life — Juvenile literature. I. Austen, Mary. II. Title.
QH48.A97 2016
578.7—d23

Manufactured in the United States of America

CPSIA Compliance Information: Batch #BW16PK: For Further Information contact Rosen Publishing, New York, New York at 1-800-237-9932

Contents

The country is a beautiful place to live.

The country is also known as a rural community.

There are fewer people living in the country than in a city. There are fewer homes and other buildings, too.

8

country

city

Homes and other buildings in the country are often far from one another. We live far from our neighbors!

Some people who live in the country work in the city. They drive a long way to work each day.

13

Some people who live in the country work on **ranches**. A ranch is a big farm where cows and horses live.

The country is a great place for horses to live. They have a lot of room to run!

We see many wild animals in the country. Owls fly in the country sky!

Field mice live in the open fields of the country. We see them when we walk around our land.

It gets very dark and quiet
in the country at night.
We see more stars
than people can in the city.

Words to Know

field mouse

ranch

Index

Websites

Due to the changing nature of Internet links, PowerKids Press has developed an online list of websites related to the subject of this book. This site is updated regularly. Please use this link to access the list: www.powerkidslinks.com/acom/ctry